To: _____

From: _____

Sisters
Copyright © 1994 by
Chatham Publications
P.O. Box 39424
Minneapolis, MN 55439

Printed in Hong Kong. All rights reserved.
Scripture quotations marked (NIV) are taken
from the HOLY BIBLE, NEW INTER-
NATIONAL VERSION. Copyright © 1973,
1978, 1984 International Bible Society.
Used by permission of Zondervan
Publishing House. Verses marked (TLB) are
taken from THE LIVING BIBLE, Copyright
© 1971. Used by permission of Tyndale
House Publishers, Inc., Wheaton, IL 60189.
No part of this book may be reproduced in
any form without written permission from
the publisher.

Product # 920
ISBN: 1-57095-502-6
10 9 8 7 6 5 4 3 2 1

Sisters

Chatham
PUBLICATIONS

For there is no friend like a sister in calm or stormy weather; to cheer one on the tedious way, to fetch one if one goes astray, to lift one if one totters down, to strengthen whilst one stands.

Christina Rossetti

God bless thy year!
Thy rest, thy travel-
ing about,
The rough, the
smooth,
The bright, the drear,
God bless thy year!

Love is a little blind; when we love someone dearly we unconsciously overlook many faults.

Beatrice Saunders

Love is patient, love is kind...Love does not delight in evil but rejoices with the truth. It always protects, always trusts, always hopes, always perseveres.

1 Corinthians 13:4, 6-7 NIV

There is no friend
like an old friend
who has shared our
morning days,
No greeting like his
welcome, no
homage like his
praise.

Oliver Wendell Holmes

You never really leave a place you love. Part of it you take with you, leaving a part of yourself behind.

May the Lord keep watch between you and me when we are away from each other.

Genesis 31:49 NIV

This is my com-
mand: Love each
other.

John 15:17 NIV

I thank my God
every time I remem-
ber you.

Philippians 1:3 NIV

I wish you love, and
strength, and faith,
and wisdom,
Goods, gold enough
to help some
needy one.
I wish you songs, but
also blessed silence,
And God's sweet
peace when every
day is done.

Dorothy Nell McDonald

So encourage each other to build each other up, just as you are already doing.

1 Thessalonians 5:11 TLB

Love...is like a beautiful flower which I may not touch, but whose fragrance makes the garden a place of delight just the same.

Helen Keller

In goodness there are all kinds of wisdom.

Euripides

She openeth her mouth with wisdom; and in her tongue is the law of kindness.

Proverbs 31:26 KJV

Human love and the delights of friendship, out of which are built the memories that endure, are also to be treasured up as hints of what shall be hereafter.

Bede Jarrett

Home is where the
heart is.

Pliny the Elder

Love is patient, love is kind. It does not envy, it does not boast, it is not proud. It is not rude, it is not self-seeking, it is not easily angered, it keeps no record of wrongs.

1 Corinthians 13:4-5 NIV

Those who love
deeply never grow
old; they may die of
old age, but they die
young.

Sir Arthur Wing Pinero

What do we live for, if not to make the world less difficult for each other?

George Eliot

The day began with
   dismal doubt,
A stubborn thing to
   put to rout;
But all my worries
   flew away
When someone
   smiled at me today.

Love makes all
hard hearts gentle.

George Herbert

How gracious he will be when you cry for help! As soon as he hears, he will answer you.

Isaiah 30:19 NIV

This is the day the Lord has made. We will rejoice and be glad in it.

Psalm 118:24 TLB

Carry each other's burdens, and in this way you will fulfill the law of Christ.

Galatians 6:2 NIV

Remember this—
that very little is
needed to make a
happy life.

Marcus Aurelius

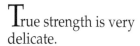

True strength is very delicate.

Nevelson

In youth we learn;
in age we under-
stand.

Von Ebner-Eschenbach

Silences make the real conversations between friends. Not the saying, but the never needing to say, is what counts.

Margaret Lee Runbeck

Be assured when you see a tear on a cheek, a heart is touched.

Time draweth wrinkles in a fair face, but addeth fresh colors to a fast friend, which neither heat, nor cold, nor misery, nor place, nor destiny, can alter or diminish.

John Lyly

I miss your hand
   beside my own,
The light touch of
   your hand,
The quick gleam in
   the eyes of you
So sure to understand.

The best things are nearest: breath in your nostrils, light in your eyes, flowers at your feet, duties at your hand, the path of God just before you.

Robert Louis Stevenson

W hat a wonderful
life I've had! I only
wish I'd realized it
sooner.

Colette

We often take for granted the very things that most deserve our gratitude.

Ozick

As outward beauty
disappears one must
hope it goes in!

Tennessee Williams

Two persons cannot
long be friends if
they cannot forgive
each other's little
failings.

Jean de La Bruyère

Still remember, she is your companion, the friend in whom you may confide at all times, and from whom you may obtain counsel and comfort.

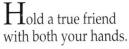

Hold a true friend
with both your hands.
Nigerian Proverb

God has given us
two hands—one to
receive with and the
other to give with.
We are not cisterns
made for hoarding;
we are channels
made for giving.

Billy Graham

Be kind and compassionate to one another, forgiving each other, just as in Christ God forgave you.

Ephesians 4:32 NIV

Here's hoping that
 on Fortune's face
You'll never see a
 frown,
And that the corners
 of your mouth
May never be turned
 down.

Lucinda May

Above all, love each other deeply, because love covers over a multitude of sins.

1 Peter 4:8 NIV

May the Lord, the God of your fathers, increase you a thousand times and bless you as he has promised!

Deuteronomy 1:11 NIV

God has not called us to see through each other, but to see each other through.

Carry each other's burdens, and in this way you will fulfill the law of Christ.

Galatians 6:2 NIV

Treat your friends
like family and your
family like friends.

I would be friends
with you and have
your love.

Shakespeare

Two are better than one...If one falls down, his friend can help him up. But pity the man who falls and has no one to help him up!

Ecclesiastes 4:9-10 NIV

The secret of life is
that it is God-given.

Love is not blind—
it sees more, not less.
But because it sees
more, it is willing to
see less.

Rabbi Julius Gordon

God grant me the Serenity to accept the things I cannot change, the Courage to change the things I can, and the Wisdom to know the difference. Amen.

I listened, motionless
and still;
And as I mounted up
the hill,
The music in my
heart I bore,
Long after it was
heard no more.

William Wordsworth

A woman who fears the Lord is to be praised.

Proverbs 31:30 NIV

I would rather walk
with God in the dark
than go alone in the
light.

Mary Gardiner Brainard

The Lord is near to all who call on him, to all who call on him in truth.

Psalm 145:18 NIV

Bless this house, O
Lord, we pray,
Make it safe by night
and day;
Bless these walls, so
firm and stout,
Keeping want and
trouble out.

Taylor

When God measures a person He puts the tape around the heart and not the head.

The best and most beautiful things in the world cannot be seen or even touched. They must be felt with the heart.

Helen Keller

Don't walk in front
of me,
I may not follow.
Don't walk behind
me,
I may not lead.
Walk beside me,
And just be my
friend.

Albert Camus

Good make thee
good as thou art
beautiful.

Alfred, Lord Tennyson

"Unbosom your-
self," said Wimsey.
"Trouble shared is
trouble halved."

Dorothy Sayers

Treasure each other
in the recognition
that we do not know
how long we shall
have each other.

Joshua Loth Liebman

I f instead of a gem,
or even a flower, we
should cast the gift
of a loving thought
into the heart of a
friend, that would be
giving as the angels
give.

George Macdonald

Happiness consists in forgetting what one gives, and remembering what one receives.

It is a beautiful necessity of our nature to love something.

Douglas Jerrold

So God created man in his own image....

Genesis 1:27 NIV

Gratitude is the
memory of the heart.

J. B. Massieu

A happy heart
makes the face
cheerful....

Proverbs 15:13 NIV

When we are tired
we are attacked by
thoughts that we
conquered long ago.

...he leads me beside
quiet waters, he
restores my soul....

Psalm 23:2-3 NIV

We must strengthen, defend, preserve and comfort each other. We must love one another.

John Winthrop

W hen one helps
another, both are
strong.

German Proverb

The soul needs
friendship, the heart
needs love.

Ed Habib

Keep your face to the sunshine and you cannot see the shadow.

Helen Keller

H
appiness is not a
state to arrive at, but a
manner of traveling.

Margaret Lee Runbeck

If you have joy in your heart it will be known by the look on your face.

I love you for putting your hand into my heaped-up heart...and for drawing out into the light all the beautiful, radiant belongings that no one else has looked quite far enough to find.

Grow old along
with me!
The best is yet to be,
The last of life for
which the first
was made:
Our times are in His
hand....

Robert Browning

Blessed are they
who are pleasant to
live with.

Out of the abun-
dance of the heart
the mouth speaketh.

Matthew 12:34 KJV

Who, being loved,
is poor?

Oscar Wilde

A friend is a person
with whom you dare
to be yourself.

Frank Crane

We have been
friends together in
sunshine and shade.

Caroline Norton

Few burdens are heavy when everyone lifts.

Carry each other's burdens, and in this way you will fulfill the law of Christ.

Galatians 6:2 NIV

Love seeks not
limits but outlets.

If there is anything better than to be loved, it is loving.

Rings and jewels
are not gifts, but
apologies for gifts.
The only gift is a
portion of thyself.

Ralph Waldo Emerson

W hen you cannot
pray as you would,
pray as you can.

Dean M. Goulburn

...Lord, teach us to
pray....

Luke 11:1 NIV

There is as much
greatness of mind in
acknowledging a good
turn as in doing it.

Seneca

All people smile in the same language.

The task ahead of us
is never as great as
the Power behind us.

I can do everything
through him who
gives me strength.

Philippians 4:13 NIV

She who wants her garden tidy does not reserve a plot for weeds.

Be happy. It's one way of being wise.

Colette

...let the righteous be glad; let them rejoice before God....

Psalm 69:3 KJV

Recall it as often as you wish, a happy memory never wears out.

Libbie Fudim

Let us be of good
cheer, remembering
that the misfortunes
hardest to bear are
those which never
come.

James Russell Lowell